MW01641054
elixir piping
and drumming
for SCQF/PDQB Exams

Elixir Piping and Drumming

Exam Excellence Programme

Excellence for Everyone

Developing pipe band drumming excellence through progressive study units, each delivered through a goal specific student task book.
Completion of each study unit prepares students for the following Scottish Credit and Qualifications Framework (SCQF) exams:

Elixir Study Unit	SCQF	PDQB (Piping and Drumming Qualifications Board)
1	-	-
2	**4**	Level 2
3	**5**	Level 3
4	**6**	Level 4
Teaching Unit 1 Lesson Diary 1	-	Tutor Certificate
Teaching Unit 2 Lesson Diary 2	-	Teacher Certificate

Each study unit consists of three sections:

Performance:
Study areas for all required performance elements

Theory:
Study areas for all required theory elements

Exam Excellence:
This section takes the form of an end of unit assessment and should be marked
A *(Achieved)* or **NA** *(Not Achieved)*
On completion, the student record should show an (**A**) against all study areas and be signed off by a tutor, ensuring the student is ready to progress to the next level.

EXAM EXCELLENCE PROGRAMME

The Drummers Launch Pad

for Complete Beginners

STUDY UNIT 1

By Elixir Piping And Drumming

First published in 2013 by Grace Note Publications
In collaboration with Elixir Piping and Drumming

2nd Edition 2016 (with revisions)

ISBN: 978- 1523892143

www.elixir.scot

A catalogue record for this book is available from the British Library

ALL TITLES FROM ELIXIR PIPING AND DRUMMING:

Early Learning Programme
Bagpipes For Beginners
Exam Repertoire Study Units 2 – 6
Study Unit 2 For Solo Pipers
Study Unit 3 For Solo Pipers
Study Unit 4 For Solo Pipers
Study Unit 5 For Solo Pipers
Study Unit 6 For Solo Pipers
Study Unit 7 For Solo Pipers
Study Unit 8 For Solo Pipers
Study Unit 9 For Solo Pipers
Study Unit 10 For Solo Pipers
Study Unit 11 For Solo Pipers
Performance Unit 1
Performance Unit 2
Performance Unit 3
Performance Unit 4
Piobaireachd Unit
Teaching Unit 1/Lesson Diary 1
Teaching Unit 2/Lesson Diary 2

The Drummers Launch Pad

Study Unit 2 For Pipe Band Drummers
Study Unit 3 For Pipe Band Drummers
Study Unit 4 For Pipe Band Drummers
Teaching Unit 1/Lesson Diary 1
Teaching Unit 2/Lesson Diary 2

Sight Reading, Study Unit 1
Sight Reading, Study Unit 2
Sight Reading, Study Unit 3
Sight Reading, Study Unit 4
Sight Reading, Study Unit 5
Sight Reading, Study Unit 6
Sight Reading, Study Unit 7
Sight Reading, Study Unit 8

About the Authors

Making a Difference

Elixir Piping and Drumming specialise in peak performance coaching for pipers, drummers and pipe bands, through the design and delivery of unique development programmes.

The Elixir Team are registered SCQF Assessors and full-time, professionally qualified and experienced piping and drumming instructors.

They passionately believe in 'Excellence for Everyone', through progressive goal setting, continual pursuit of excellence, and peak performance.

Your Goal is Our Goal.

Acknowledgements
To all our students, and to all students who embark on the SCQF/PDQB syllabus, who challenge us to give our best, find a better way, and continue to learn and grow, as they explore their own potential;
To family, friends and the many great people along the way who encourage, support and genuinely make a difference to our lives;
To Gonzalo Mazzei and Margaret Bennett for starting us on our own journey of excellence;

Thank you for all the ways in which you inspire us in our own continual pursuit of excellence.

"Everything is Practice" *- Pele*

Excellence is not a Gift, **Excellence is Practice**

Practice does not make Perfect - **Practice makes Habit**

Bad Practice = **Bad Habit = Bad Playing**

Good Practice = **Good Habit = Good Playing**

Become What You Practice

THE ICEBERG *(The Secret of Success)*

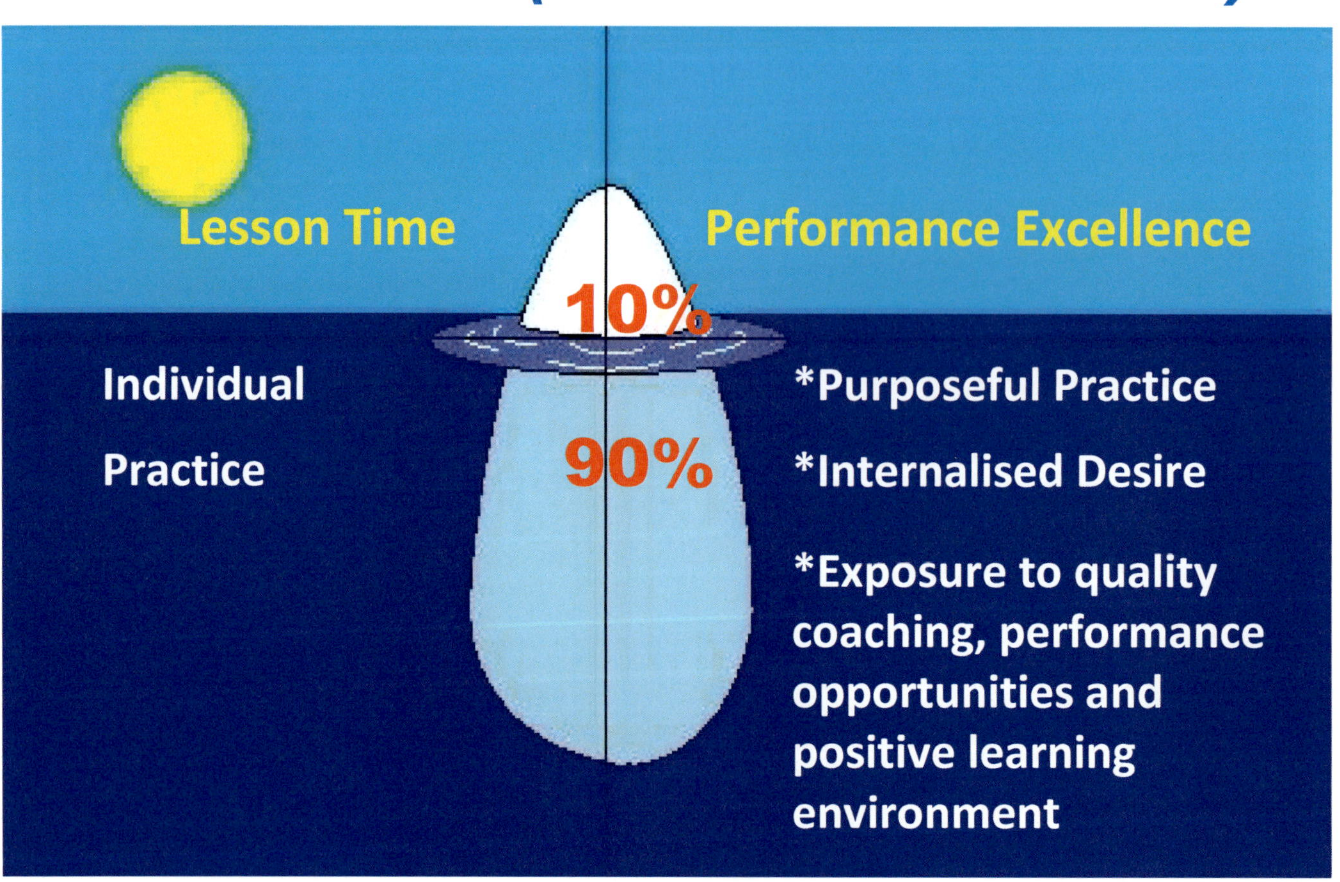

CONTENTS

Performance and Theory Study Units should be studied/taught in tandem

Suggested Teaching Schedule

Course Introduction Date: A / NA	Lesson 1 Date: A / NA	Lesson 2 Date: A / NA	Lesson 3 Date: A / NA	Lesson 4 Date: A / NA
Lesson 5 Date: A / NA	Lesson 6 Date: A / NA	Lesson 7 Date: A / NA	Lesson 8 Date: A / NA	Lesson 9 Date: A / NA
Lesson 10 Date: A / NA	Revision Lesson Date: A / NA	Revision Lesson Date: A / NA	Lesson 11 Date: A / NA	Lesson 12 Date: A / NA
Lesson 13 Date: A / NA	Lesson 14 Date: A / NA	Revision Lesson Date: A / NA	Lesson 15 Date: A / NA	Revision Lesson Date: A / NA

**Suggested Teaching Schedule*
20x ½ hour lessons, TOTAL 10 hours
THIS DOES NOT INCLUDE REQUIRED INDIVIDUAL PRACTICE AND STUDY TIME

A metronome is recommended as a useful practice tool, to gauge progress and ensure tasks have been mastered to the correct speed.
All exercises should begin at 60BPM and rise to 80BPM when mastered, maintaining clarity.

Page	Lesson	A/NA
3	Technique and Repertoire	

PERFORMANCE

PROGRESS CHART

TASK	Remarks	A/NA
Tap it Out		
Absolutely Buzzing		
Rolling Along **5 Stroke Roll**		
Rolling Along **7 Stroke Roll**		
2/4 March		
Flick some Flams		
3/4 March		
Rolling Along **9 Stroke Roll**		
4/4 March		
Rolling Along **3 Pace Roll**		

LESSON 1 — TIME TO LAUNCH

Holding the Sticks

Left hand: palm facing upwards, stick resting on 3rd (ring) finger, under thumb and supported by index and middle finger

Right Hand: palm facing down, gripped between thumb and index finger, supported by ring and pinky finger

Tap It Out

Striking the pad (*single stroke*) is known as a 'tap'.

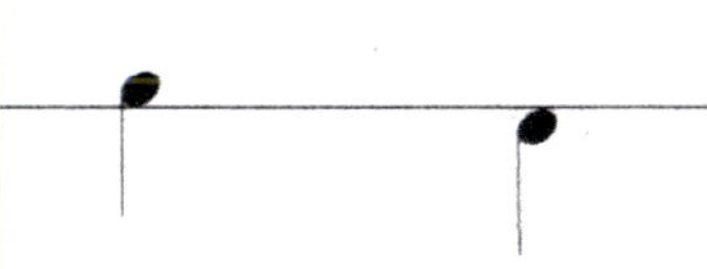

TASK Practice and master the following exercises

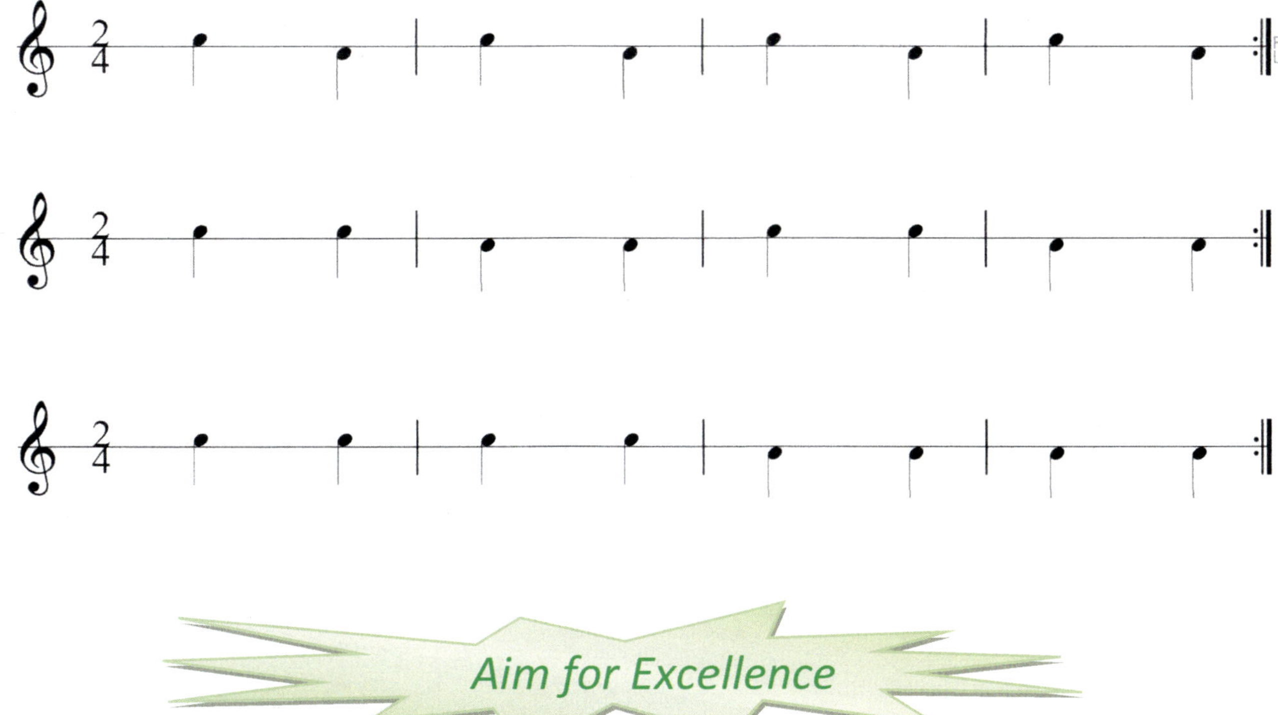

Aim for Excellence

Aim for Excellence

THE LONG AND SHORT OF IT

Dot and Cut: simply means Long and Short

TASK Practice and master the following exercises

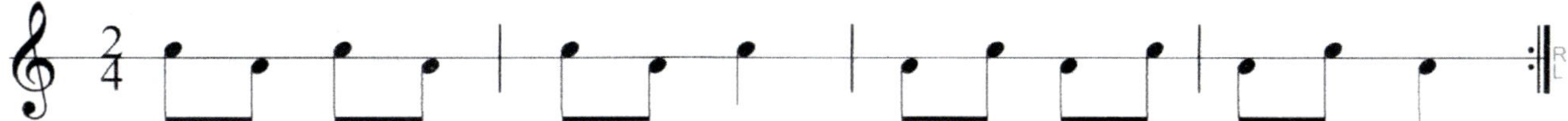

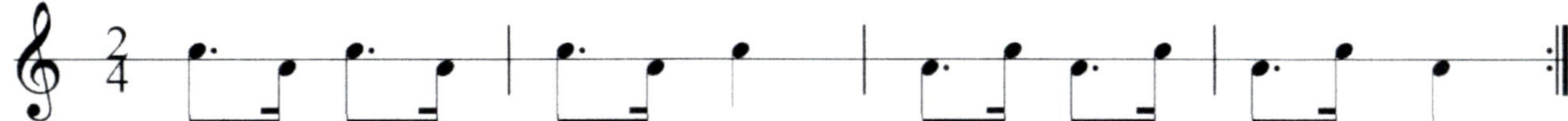

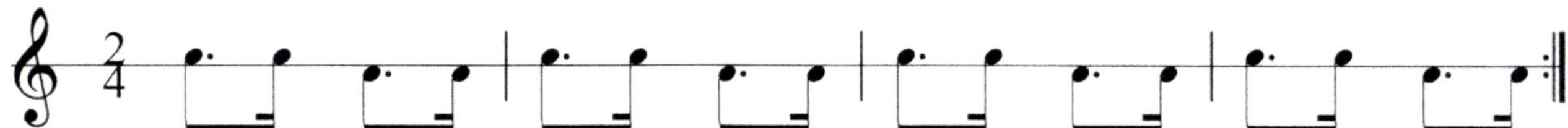

Aim for Excellence

LESSON 2 ABSOLUTELY BUZZING

There is only one other type of stroke, known as the 'buzz'.

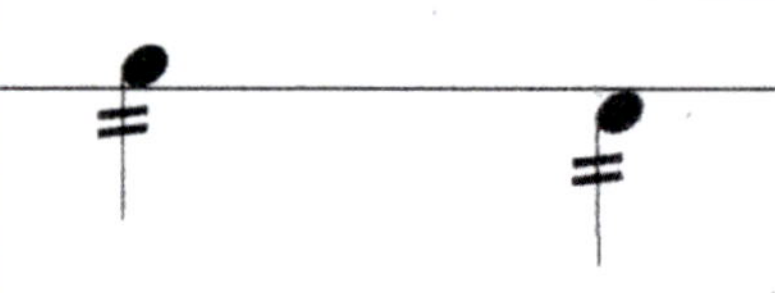

BUZZ: add a little more pressure to each stroke, so you can hear a buzz sound *(this is the stick striking more than once)*

TASK Practice and master the following exercises

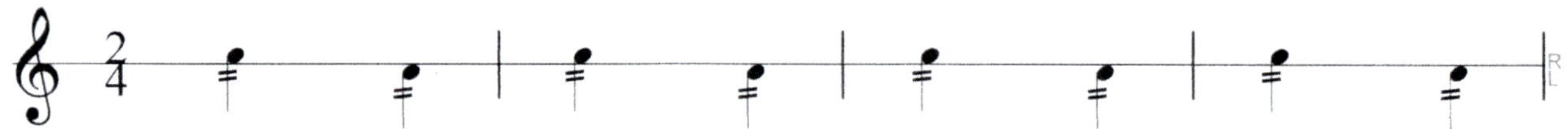

Taps and Buzzes

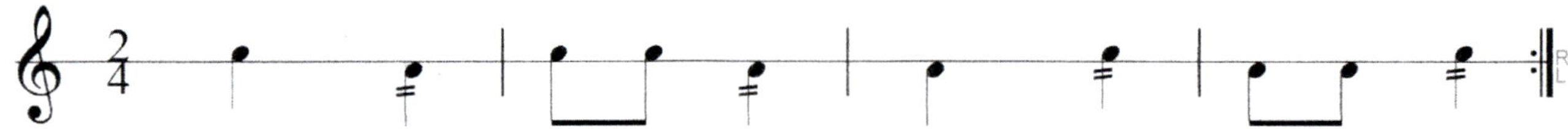

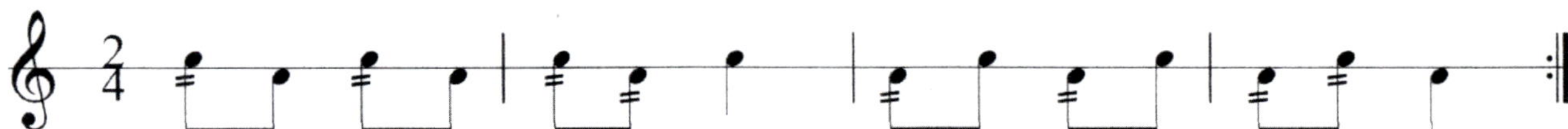

Aim for Excellence

STUDY AREA 1 – TECHNIQUE AND REPERTOIRE

LESSON 3 ROLLING ALONG

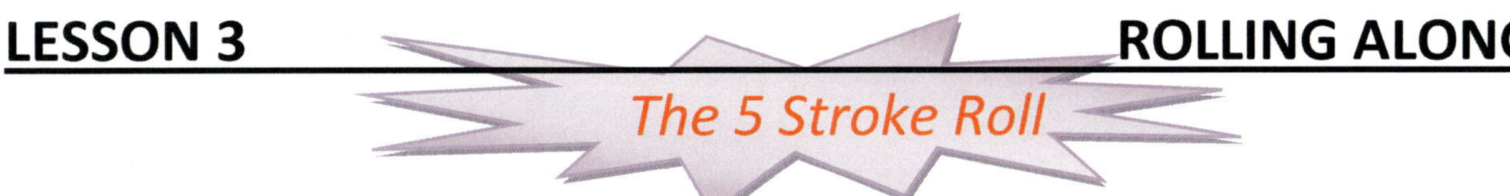

Buzz Buzz Tap

Primary Strokes

Open

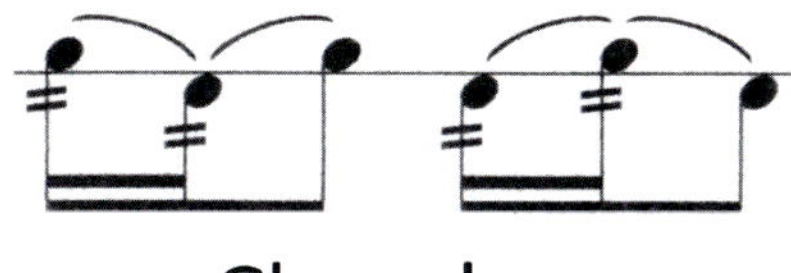

Closed

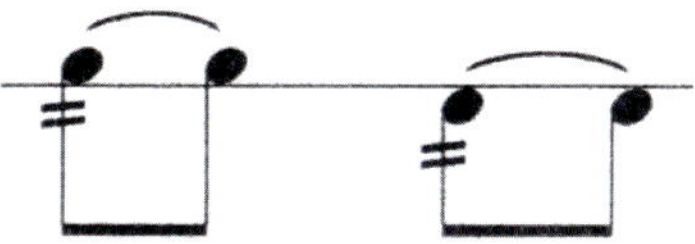

Abbreviated

(this is how the 5 Stroke Roll appears in the music)

TASK Practice and master the following exercises

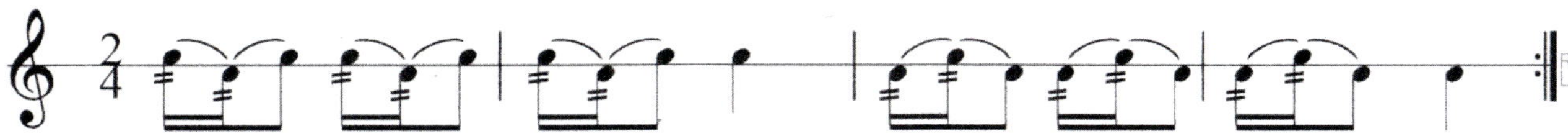

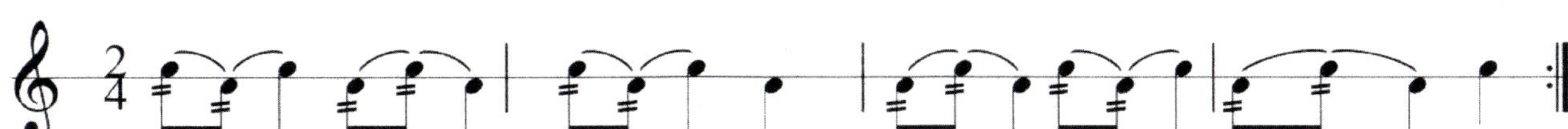

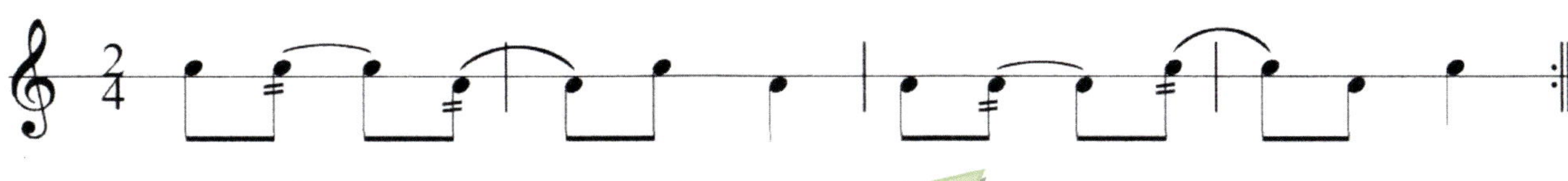

Aim for Excellence

LESSON 4 ROLLING ALONG

The 7 Stroke Roll

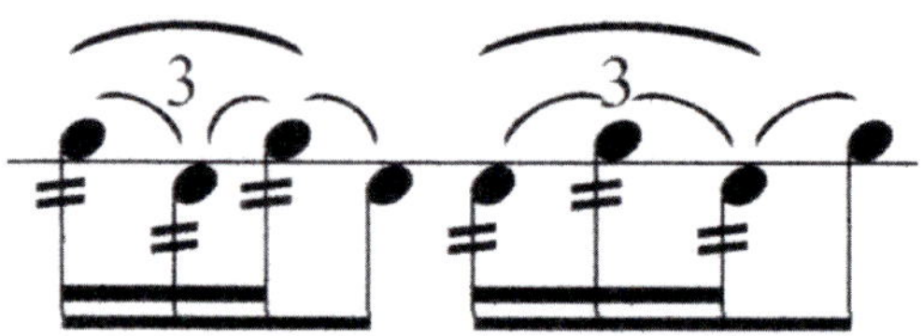

Buzz Buzz Buzz Tap Buzz Buzz Buzz Tap

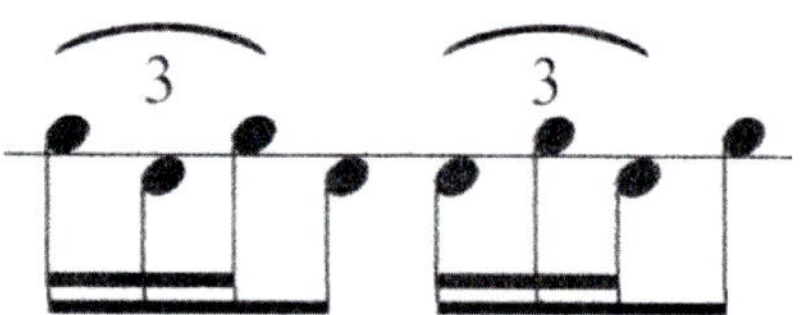

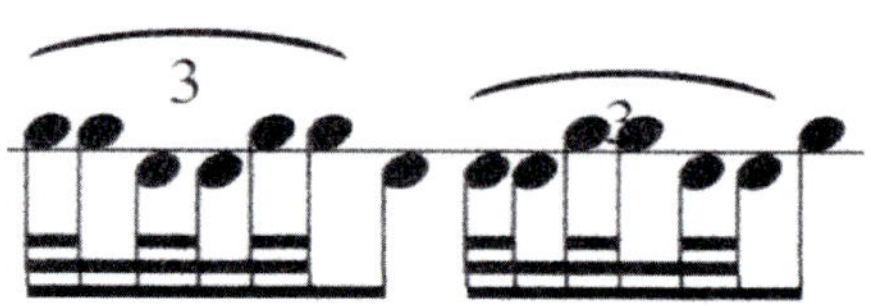

Primary Strokes

Open

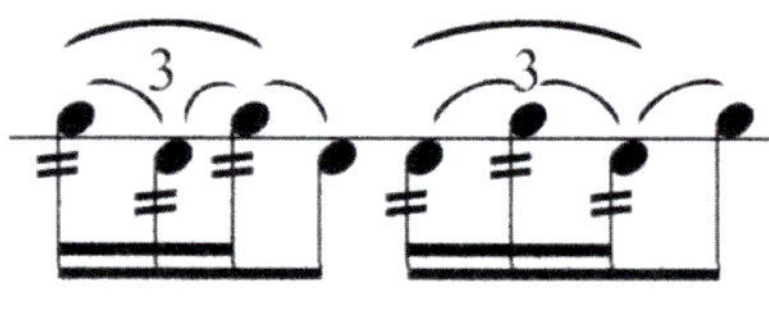

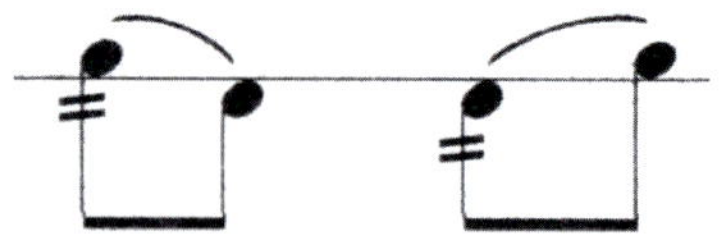

Closed

Abbreviated

(this is how the 7 Stroke Roll appears in the music)

TASK Practice and master the following exercises

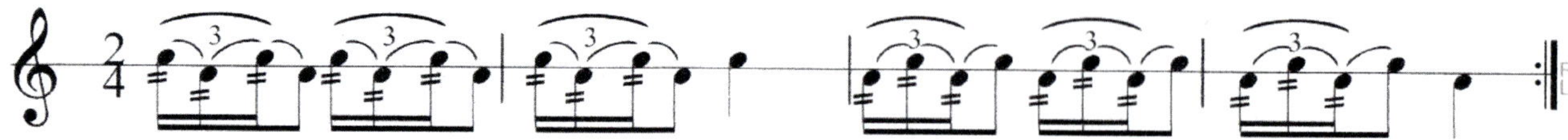

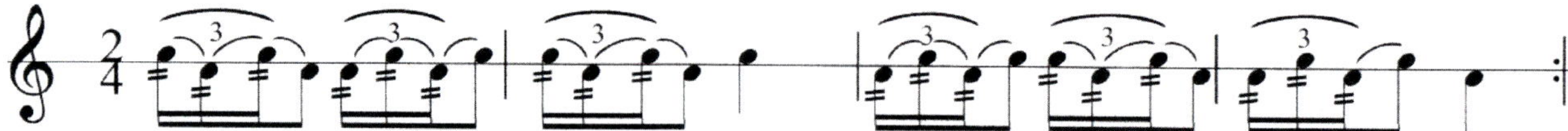

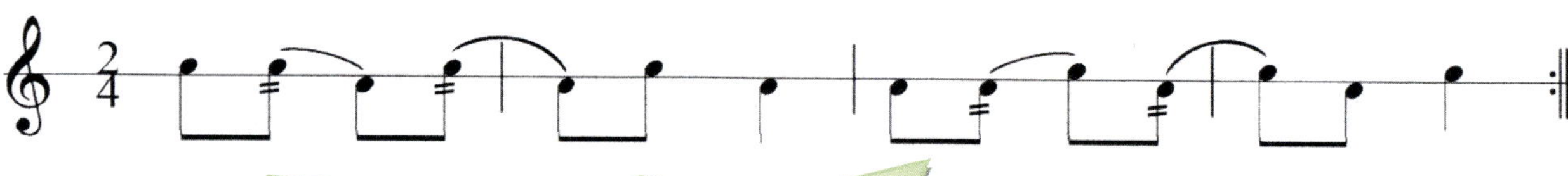

Aim for Excellence

LESSON 5 **2/4 MARCH**

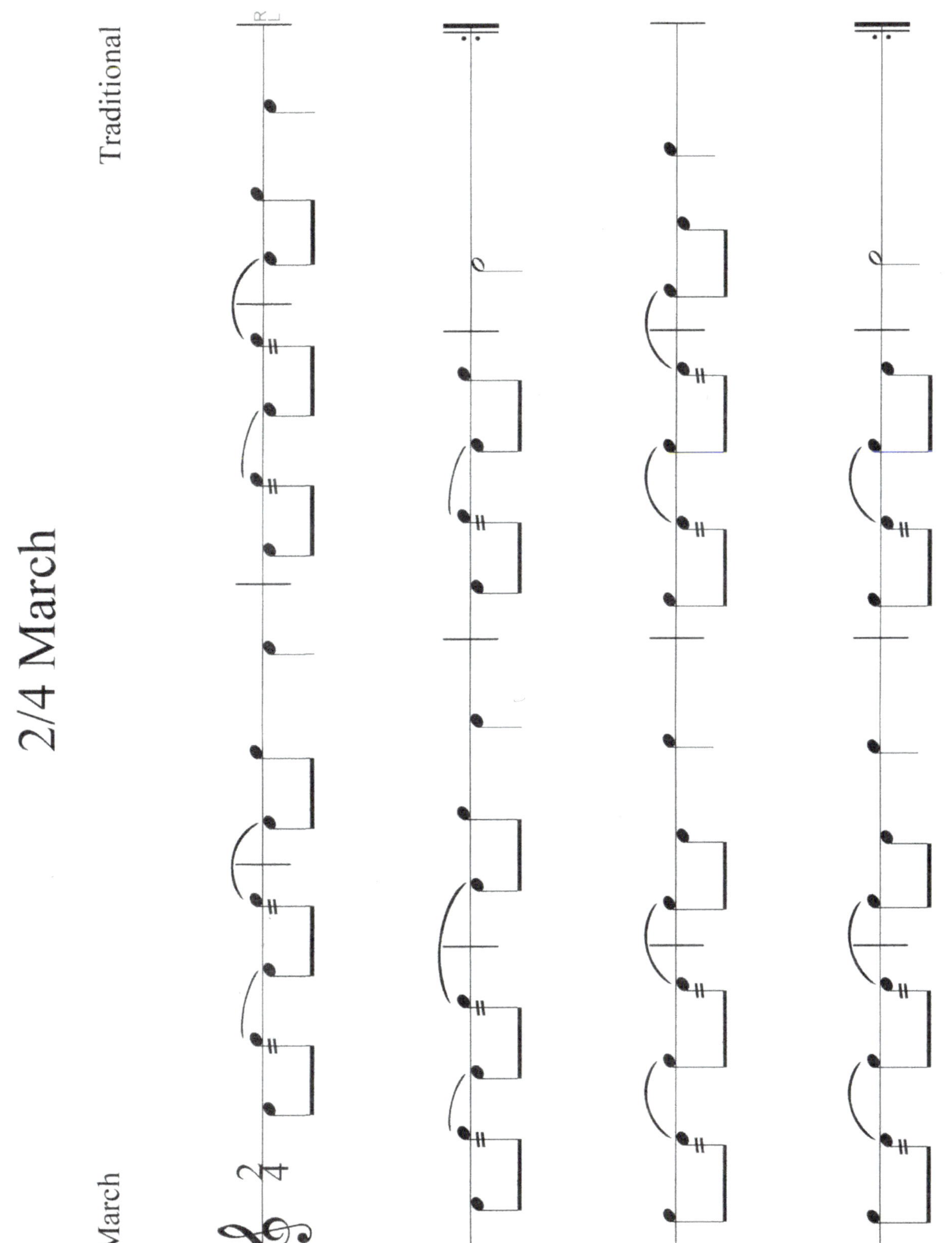

LESSON 6 — FLICK SOME FLAMS

'Flams' are two strokes together,
a soft stroke momentarily before a strong stroke,
that make a 'plup' sound.

Right Hand Flam — Left Hand Low/soft
Right Hand High/strong

Left Hand Flam — Right Hand Low/soft
Left Hand High/strong

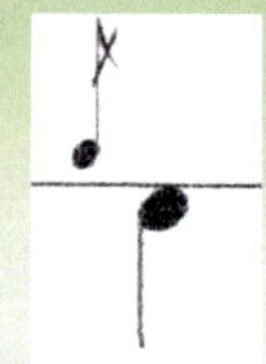

TASK — Practice and master the following exercises

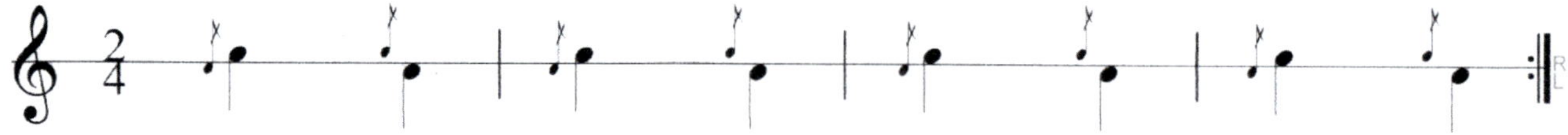

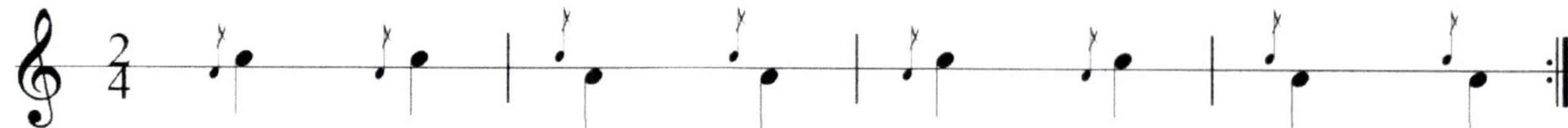

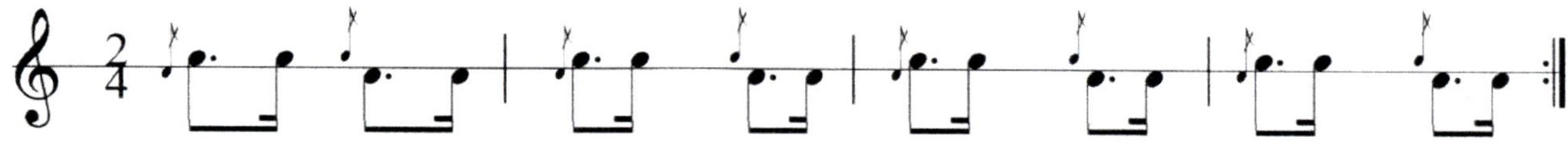

Aim for Excellence

LESSON 7 **3/4 MARCH**

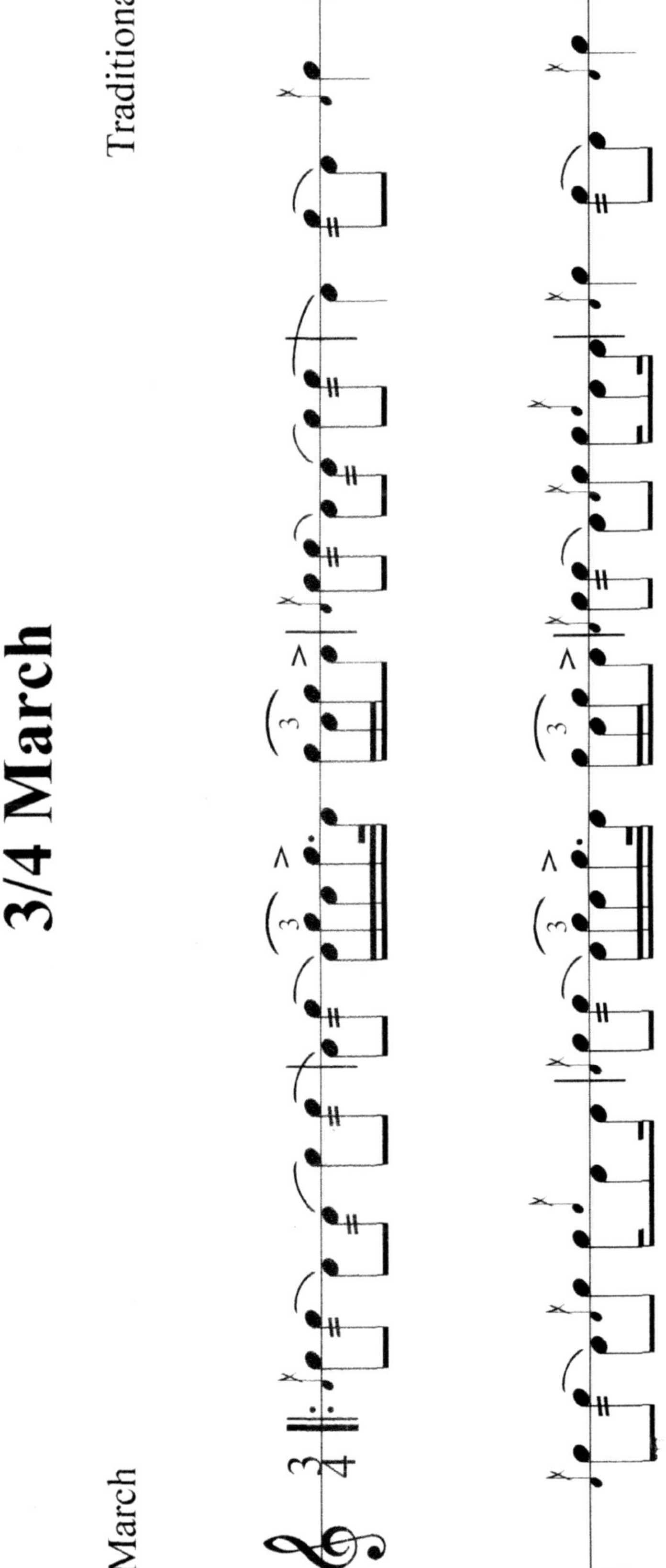

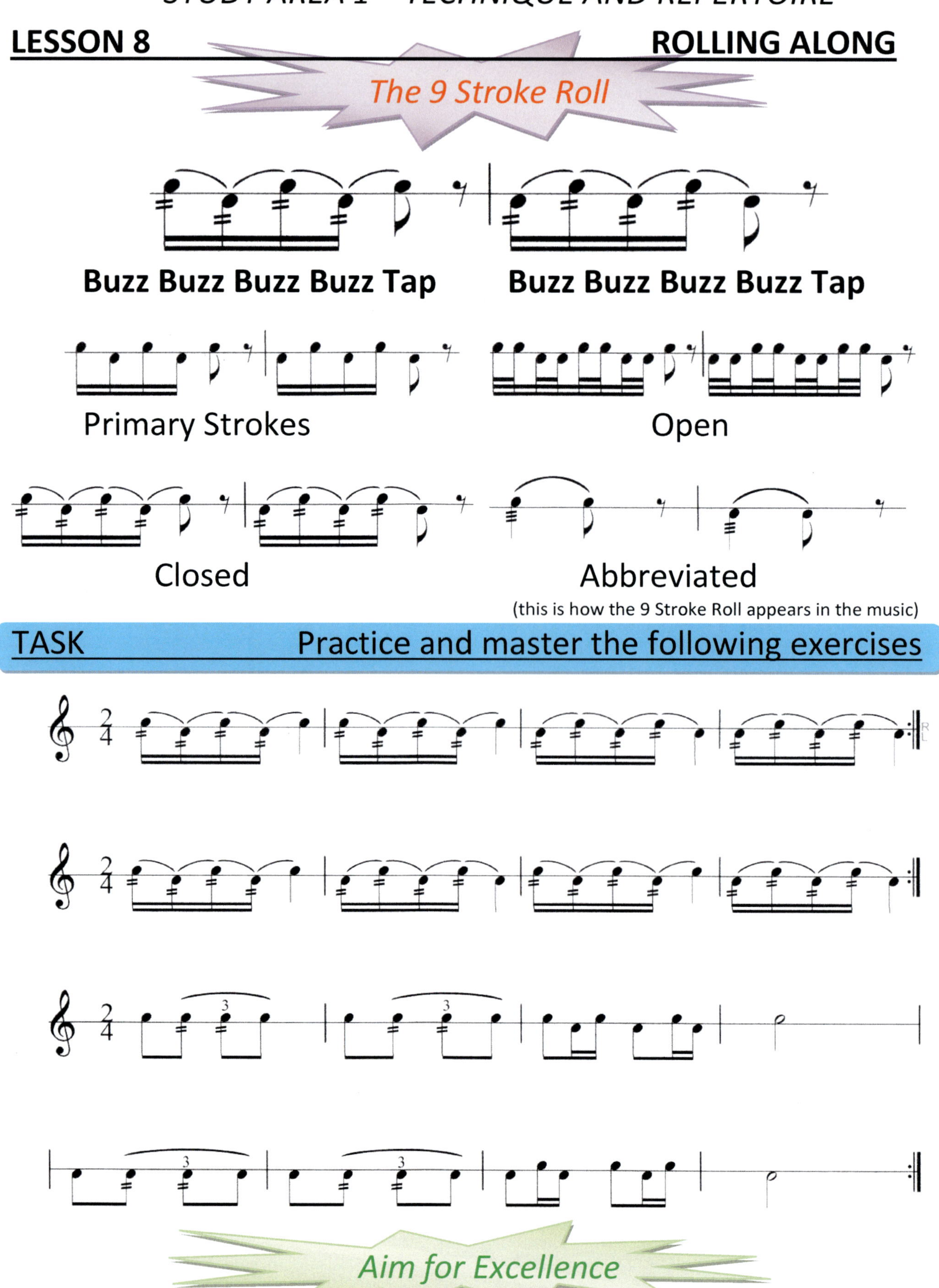
LESSON 8
ROLLING ALONG
The 9 Stroke Roll
Buzz Buzz Buzz Buzz Tap
Buzz Buzz Buzz Buzz Tap
Primary Strokes
Open
Closed
Abbreviated
(this is how the 9 Stroke Roll appears in the music)
TASK
Practice and master the following exercises
Aim for Excellence

LESSON 9 **4/4 MARCH**

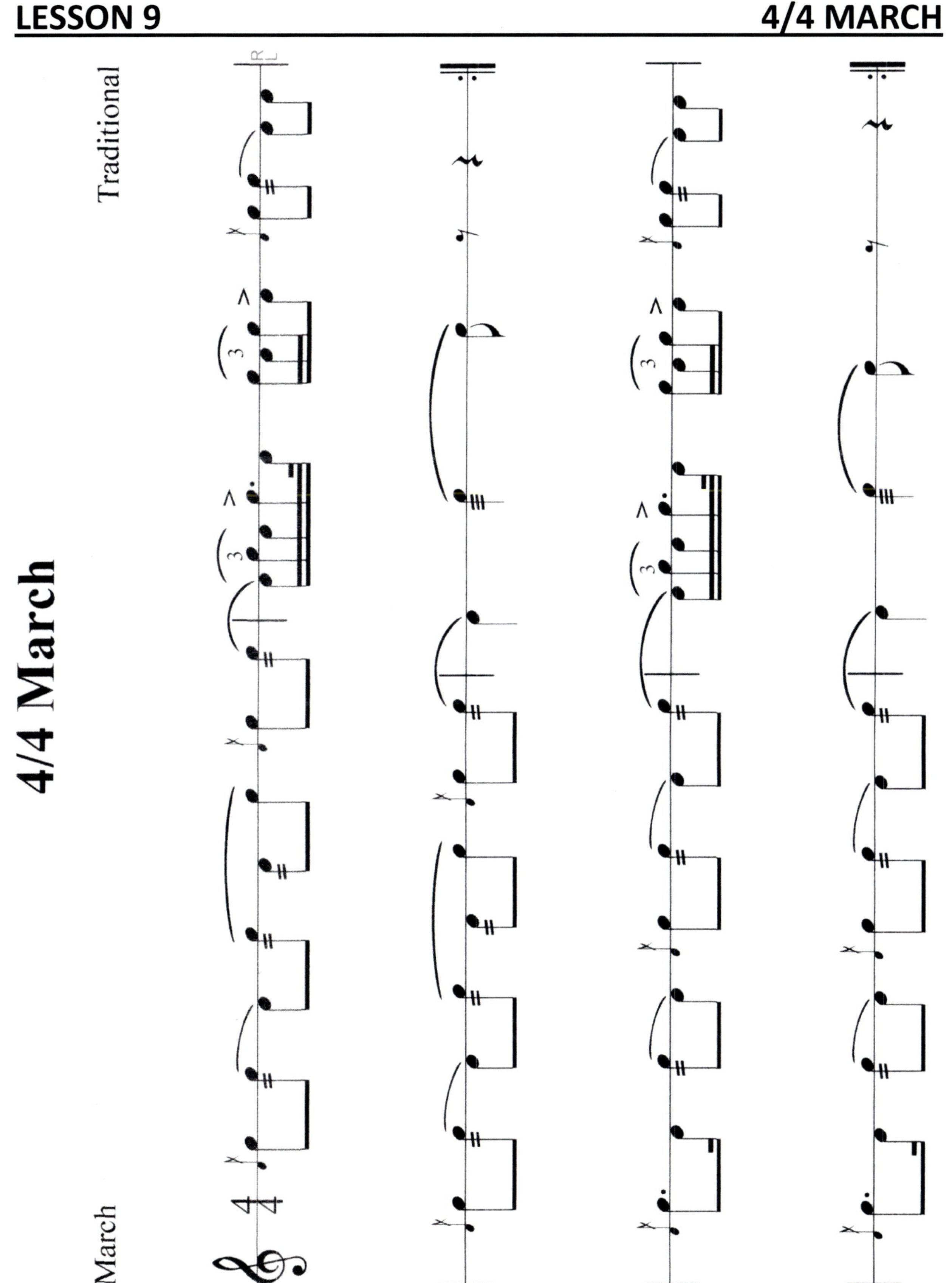

LESSON 10 ROLLING ALONG

The 3 Pace Roll

Pipe bands usually start with 2 introductory **3 Pace Rolls,** although this is not shown in the scores

TASK Practice and master the following exercise

This is a rest – count 1 before starting the next bar

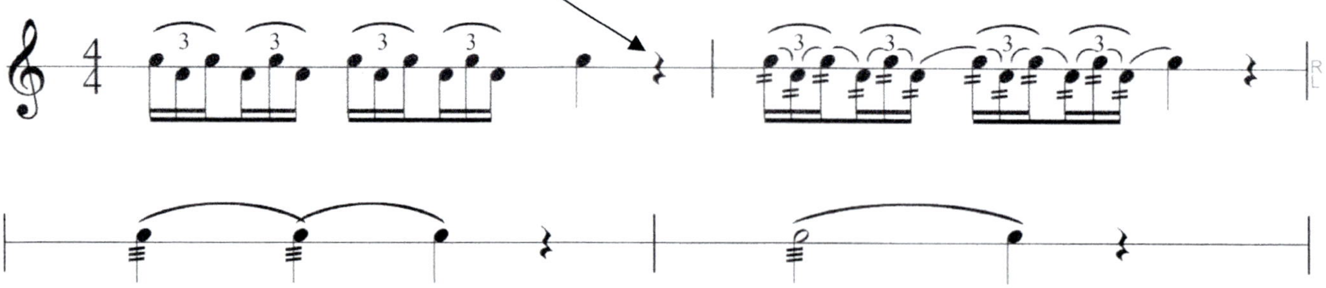

TASK
Practice the course repertoire with introductory 3 pace rolls

Aim for Excellence

EFFECTIVE PRACTICE

10 minutes EFFECTIVE PRACTICE
is **better than**
10 hours practicing mistakes

The Learning Process

- Learn *(technique & timing)*
- Memorise
- Perfect and transfer to drum

Method

- Phrase by phrase until correct, complete and memorised

Good Practice

- Goal specific
- Disciplined
- Time efficient

Always aim for **accuracy** and **perfection**

Practicing what you're good at keeps you the same,
Practicing what you're bad at **makes you better**
- fix mistakes, don't repeat them

STUDY AREA 1 – TECHNIQUE AND REPERTOIRE

TECHNIQUE DAILY WORKOUT

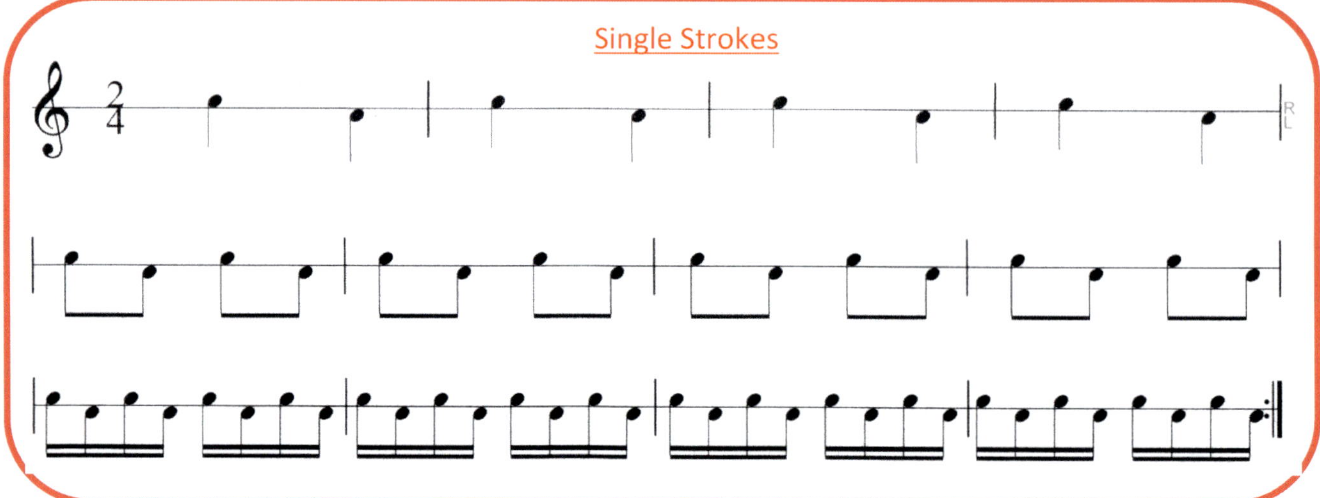

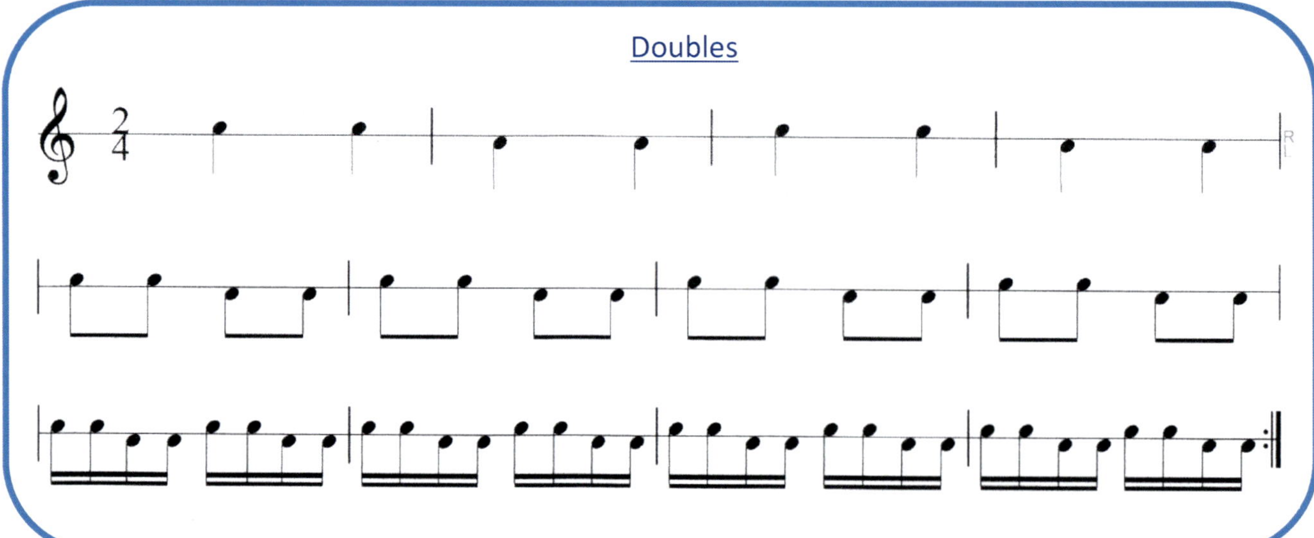

5 Stroke Roll

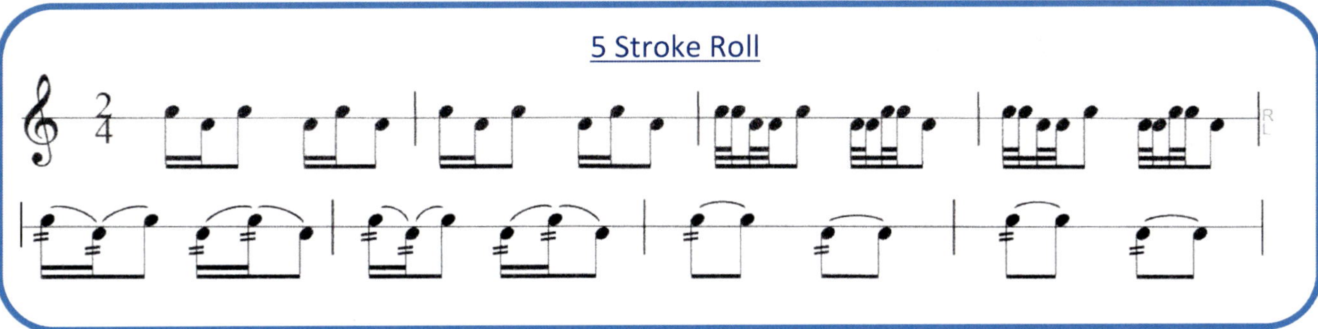

7 Stroke Roll

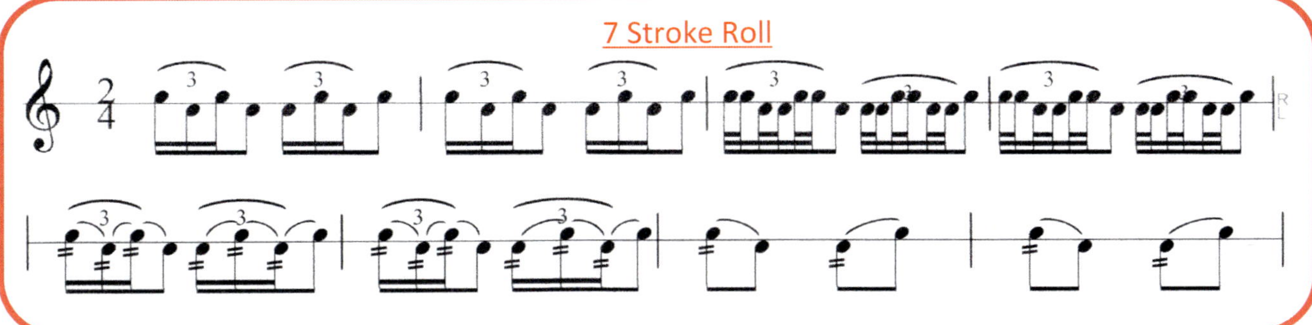

9 Stroke Roll

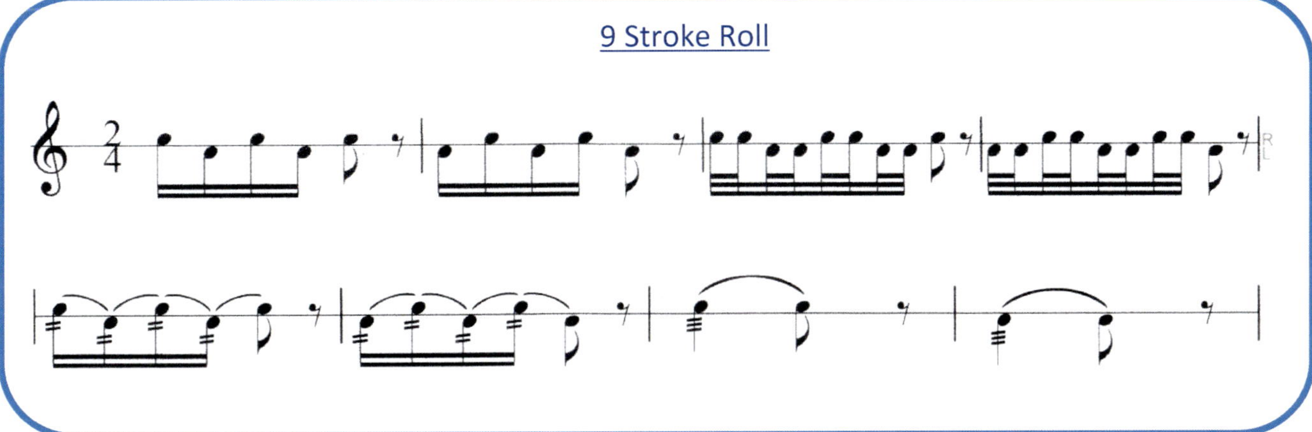

3 Pace Roll

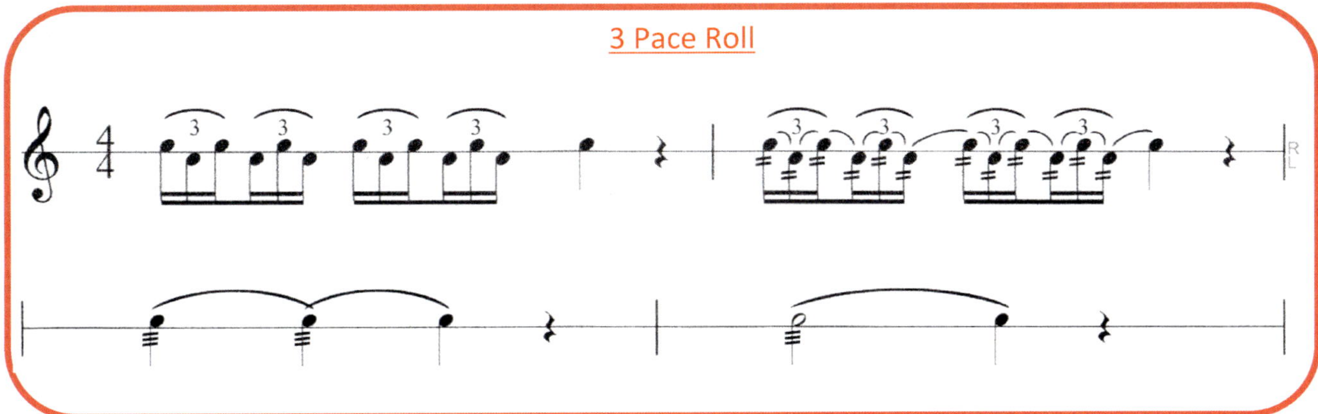

PROGRESS CHART

Tune	*Correct on Pad*	*Correct and Memorised on Pad*	*Correct and Memorised on Drum*
Daily Workout			*X*
2/4 March *(with 3 pace rolls)*			
3/4 March *(with 3 pace rolls)*			
4/4 March *(with 3 pace rolls)*			

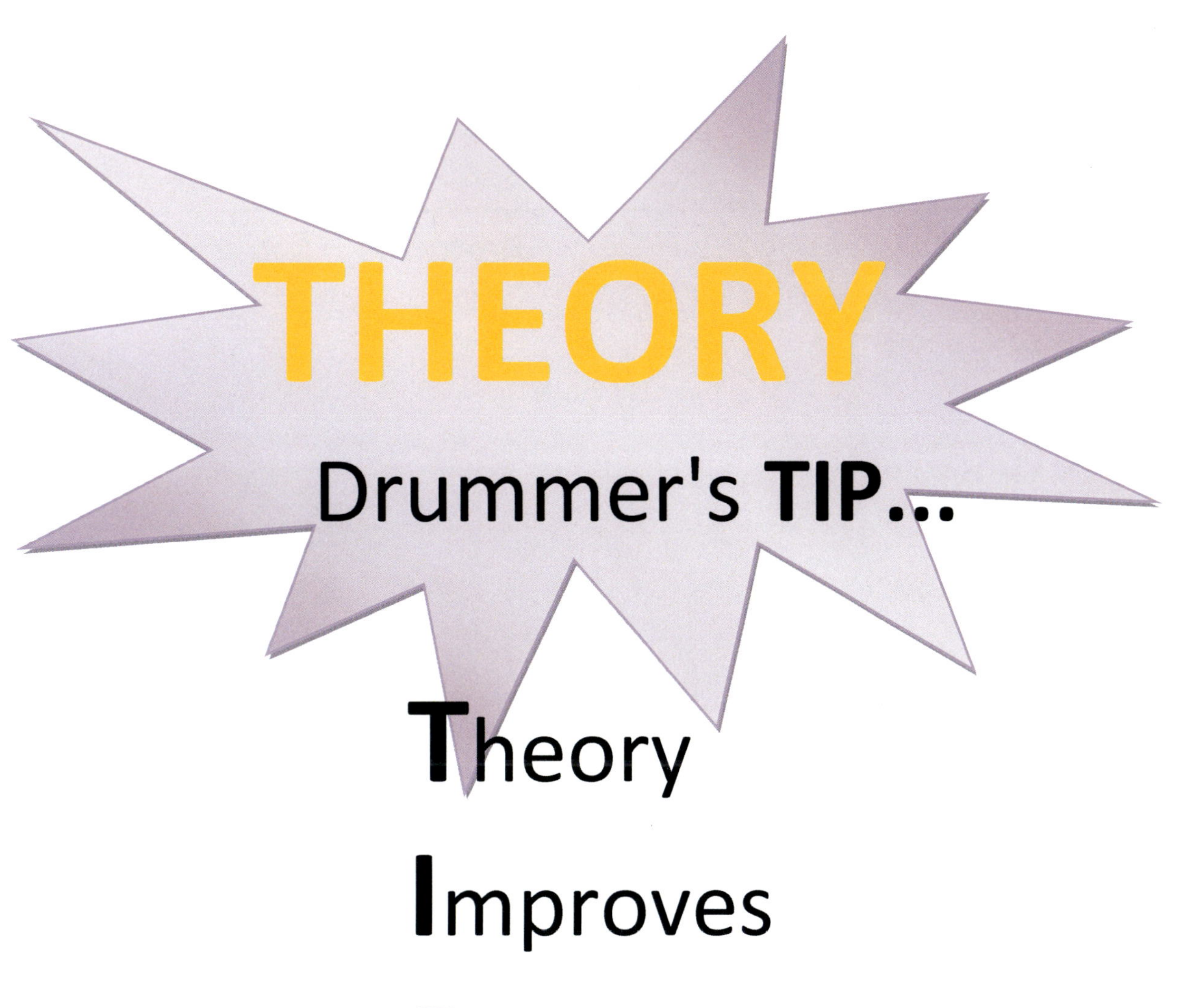

Theory

Improves

Playing

All theory tasks are recommended as homework, to make effective use of lesson time

A music manuscript book is recommended for additional practice

Page	Lesson	A/NA
21	Music Notation	
27	Music Writing	
30	Instrument Care and Maintenance	

THEORY

PROGRESS CHART

TASK	Remarks	A/NA
Reading the Stave		
Note Value Table		
Write the Notes		
Monotone Rhythms		
Note Value Table		
Time Signatures		
Writing Technique		
Technique Challenge		
Identify time signatures		
Place Bar Lines		
Know your Instrument		
Daily Checks		

LESSON 11 READING THE STAVE

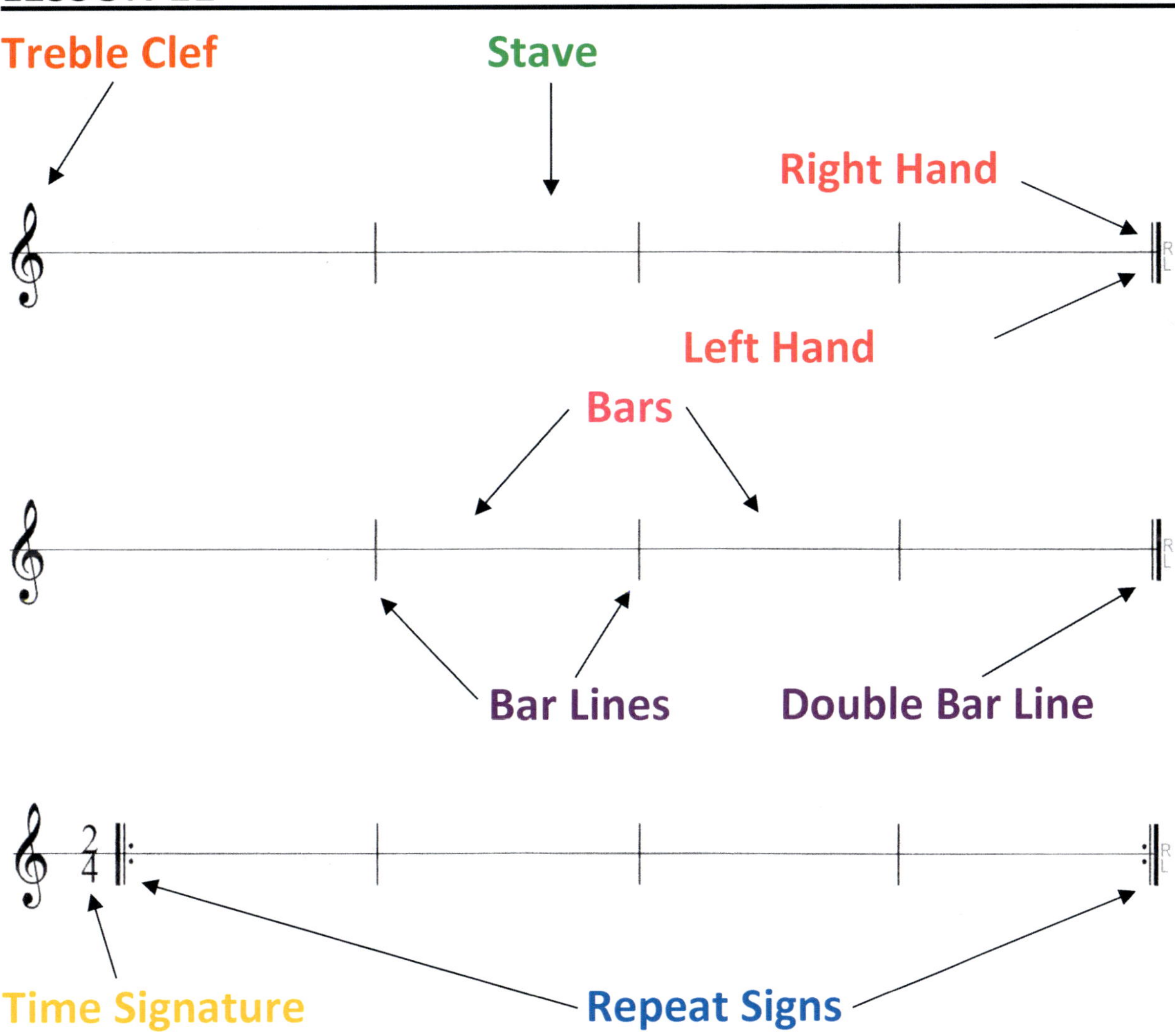

- **Stave** - 5 lines music is written on
- **Treble Clef** - Starts every line
- **Bar Lines** - Split the stave into equal sections
- **Bars** – The name for these sections
- **Double Bar Line** – Ends the section
- **Repeat Signs** - Two dots with a double bar line
- **Time Signature** - The two numbers at the start

Aim for Excellence

NOTE VALUE TABLE

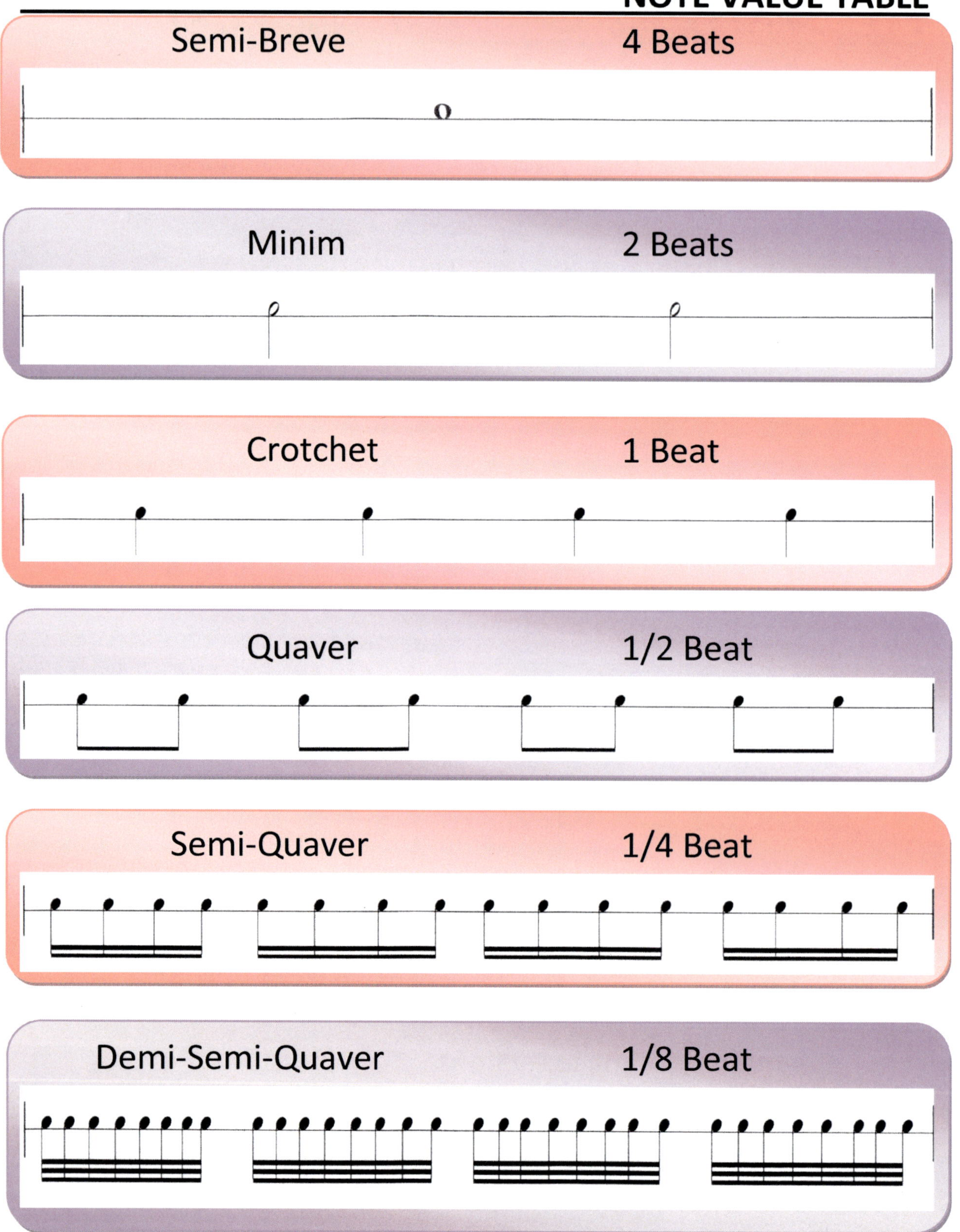

TASK

- Study the Note Value Table
- Practice writing out the Note Value Table, until correct from memory

Name/Value ______________________________

Note ______________________________

Name/Value ______________________________

Notes ______________________________

Name/Value ______________________________

Notes ______________________________

Name/Value ______________________________

Notes ______________________________

Name/Value ______________________________

Notes ______________________________

Name/Value ______________________________

Notes ______________________________

TASK

Complete the following and draw the note on the stave:

e.g. 1 Beat = Crotchet

1. 1/2 Beat =

2. 2 Beats =

3. 1/4 Beat =

4. 4 Beats =

5. 1/8 Beat =

6. 1 Beat =

Aim for Excellence

LESSON 12 — TIME SIGNATURES

Time Signature: two numbers that come after the **Treble Clef**

It shows:

Top number = how many beats in a bar

Bottom number = crotchet beats

TASK

Write 4 bars of monotone rhythms in the following time signatures

2
4 = **2** beats in a bar

3
4 = **3** beats in a bar

4
4 = **4** beats in a bar

Aim for Excellence

TIME SIGNATURES

TASK

Identify the correct time signatures of the following:

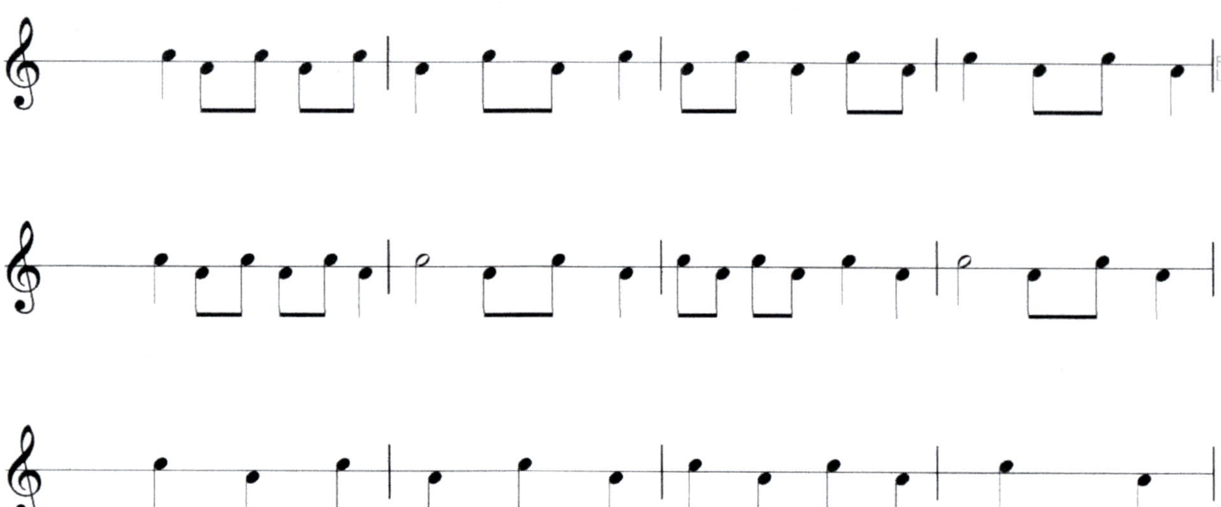

TASK

Place bar lines according to the time signature

Aim for Excellence

LESSON 13 TECHNIQUE

TASK

Copy the following technique until correct from memory

5 Stroke Roll *(primary strokes, open, closed, abbreviated)*

7 Stroke Roll *(primary strokes, open, closed, abbreviated)*

9 Stroke Roll *(primary strokes, open, closed, abbreviated)*

Flams

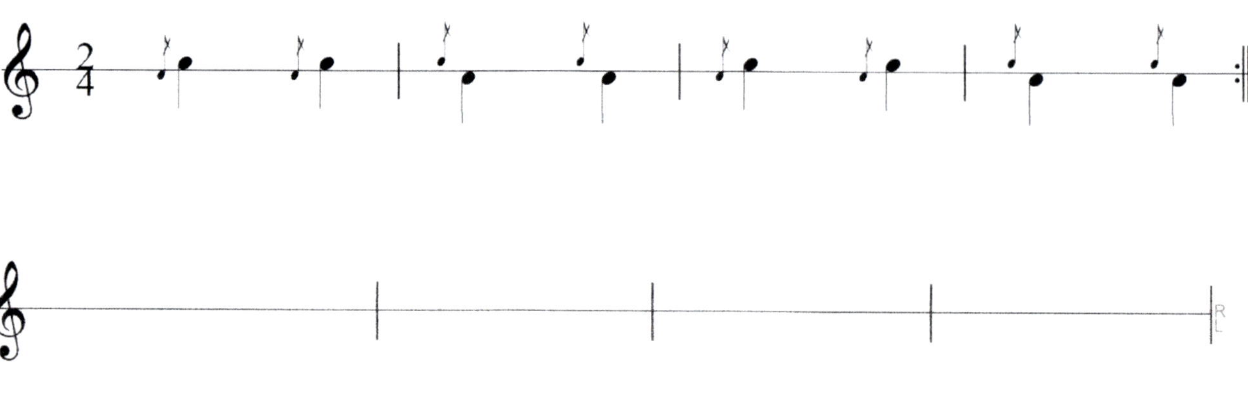

STUDY AREA 2 – MUSIC WRITING

TECHNIQUE CHALLENGE

TASK

Write the following from memory:

1. Right handed flam
2. 9 stroke roll

3. 7 stroke roll on the right hand
4. 5 Stroke Roll on the Left Hand

5. Closed 5 Stroke Roll
6. Open 5 Stroke Roll, hand to hand

7. 9 Stroke Roll – Primary Strokes
8. Closed 7 stroke roll

9. Open 9 Stroke Roll
10. Hand to hand flams

Aim for Excellence

LESSON 14 **INTRODUCTION**

Know Your Instrument

Identify these parts on your drum

Shell	Carry Hook/Harness Bracket	Tension Bolts
Top Snare	Top Head	Top Counter Hoop
Bottom Snare	Bottom Head	Bottom Counter Hoop
Snare Guards		

Daily Checks

Daily Checks for a Well Maintained Instrument

Drum = clean and dry

Tension bolts = well lubricated and rust-free

Snares = no loose or broken strands

Skins = no tears

Counter Hoops = level and good condition

Hardware = no splits or cracks

ORAL TASK	A/NA
Identify the main parts of your instrument	
Explain how to keep instrument well maintained	

Aim for Excellence

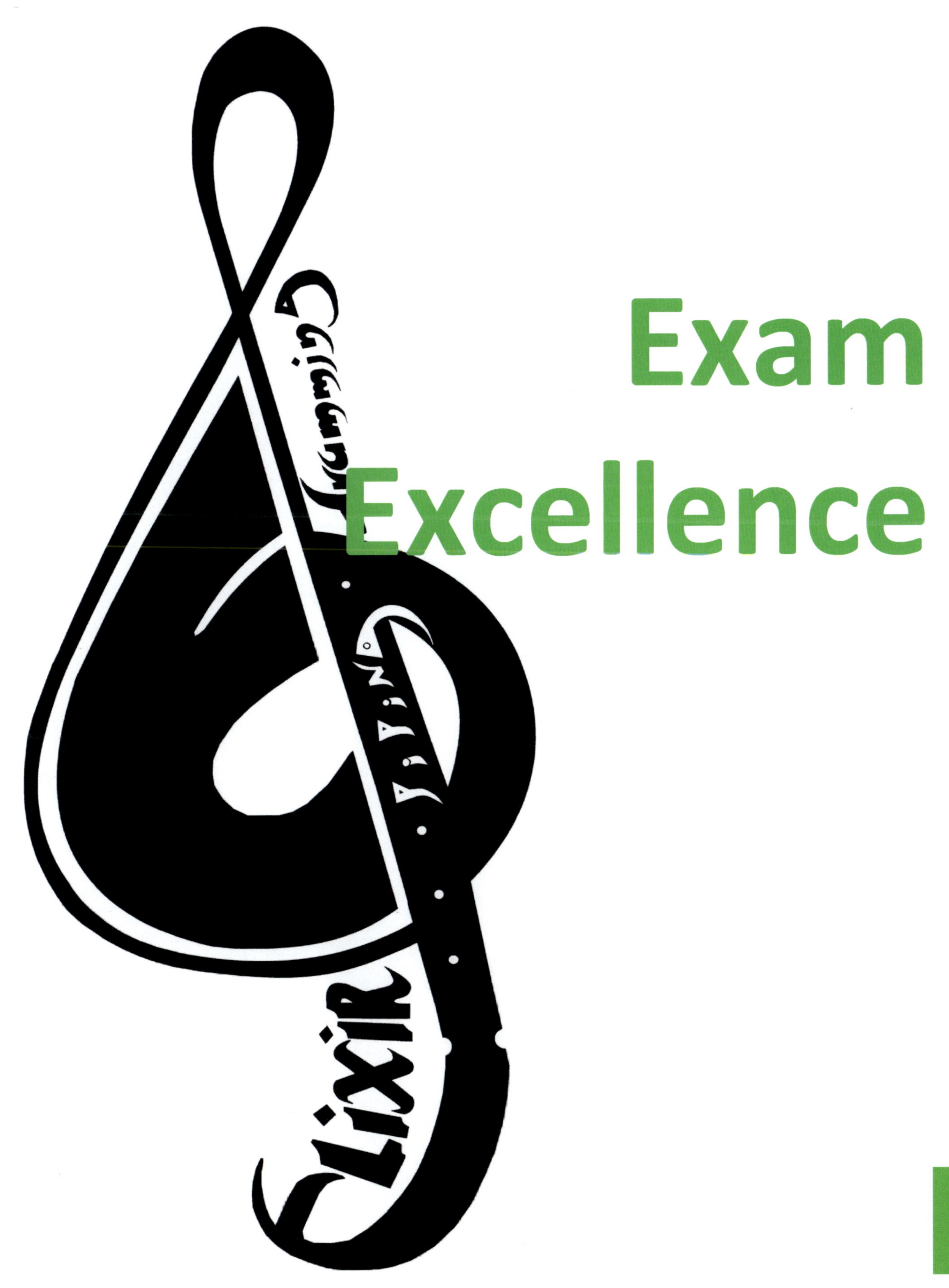

Exam Excellence

FINAL TASK

- Answer **instrument care and maintenance** questions
- Perform **technique** on the practice pad
- Perform **repertoire** on the **drum**

  (correct from memory)

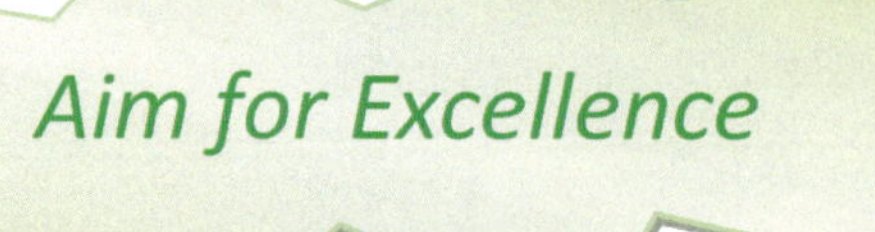

PERFORMANCE

TECHNIQUE	A/NA
Tap	
Buzz	
5 Stroke Roll – Primary Strokes, Open, Closed, abbreviated	
7 Stroke Roll – Primary Strokes, Open, Closed, abbreviated	
9 Stroke Roll – Primary Strokes, Open, Closed, abbreviated	
3 Pace Roll – Open and Closed	
Flams	
Remarks	

PIECE 1 – 2/4 March	A/NA
Remarks	
PIECE 2 – 3/4 March	
Remarks	
PIECE 3 – 4/4 March	
Remarks	

EXAM EXCELLENCE

STUDENT RECORD

Date	Study Area	Complete/Remarks	A/NA
	PERFORMANCE		
	1. Technique and Repertoire		
	THEORY		
	1. Music Notation		
	2. Music Writing		
	3. Maintenance		

Name:____________________________ **All Study Areas:** A / NA

Date:____________________ **Signed:**____________________________

AIM FOR EXCELLENCE

Made in the USA
Columbia, SC
30 October 2018